EPIDEMIC, PANDEMIC,

SHOULD I CALL THE MEDIC?

BIOLOGY BOOKS FOR KIDS

Children's Biology Books

BABY PROFESSOR
EDUCATION KIDS

Speedy Publishing LLC
40 E. Main St. #1156
Newark, DE 19711
www.speedypublishing.com

In this book, we're going to talk about epidemics and pandemics. So, let's get right to it!

WHAT IS AN EPIDEMIC?

When a very large population gets sick at the same time with an infectious disease, it's called an epidemic. For example, in 1867, over 3,000 people in New Orleans died from contracting yellow fever.

WHAT STARTS AN EPIDEMIC?

An epidemic can be started in numerous ways. Lack of sanitary conditions is one of the major causes, but there are other reasons as well.

Garbage scattered on street.

Wars and Natural Disasters

Floods, earthquakes, and other natural disasters can bring on the conditions for an epidemic to start. Wars and other violent conflicts can also be the cause. These conditions bring risks, such as water or food that's infected or introduction of new diseases. When people are going through these types of highly stressful situations, their immune systems become compromised making them more susceptible to sickness.

Flood of muddy water.

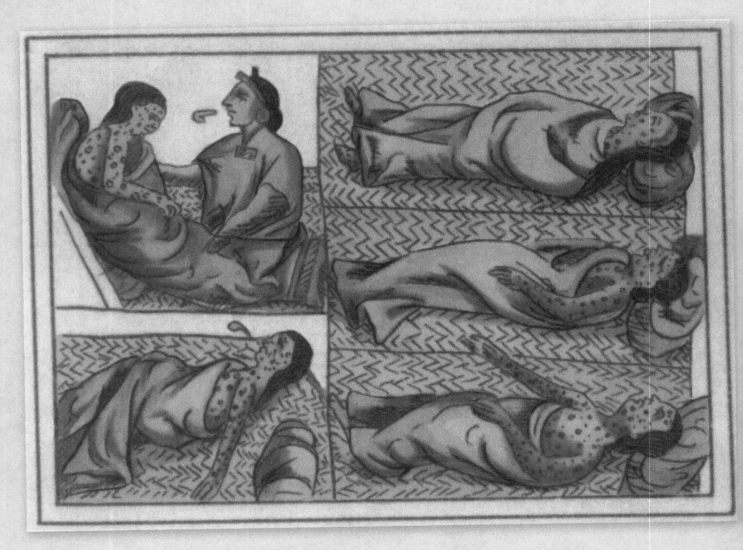

Smallpox was introduced into Mexico by the Spanish expedition of Panfilo de Narvaez

Introduction of a Disease into a Geographic Area

Sometimes diseases haven't been introduced into a specific geographic area so when they are brought there, the population doesn't have any natural immunity to them. For example, when the Europeans came to the Americas, they brought smallpox with them. Entire populations of Native Americans were destroyed by the disease, because they were never exposed to it prior to the Europeans arriving.

Lower Immunity to a Disease

At times, when people are always hungry or when they suffer from poor nutrition, these factors can cause them to have a lower level of immunity.

When a disease strikes, they can't resist it.

Homeless woman sitting alone on ground.

Infected Sources of Food or Water

If the sources of food or drinking water get infected, then this can sometimes be the start of an epidemic. Sometimes drinking water for a city can become contaminated, causing huge numbers of people to get sick at the same time.

Dirty brown water running from a filthy faucet.

A Disease Becomes More Virulent

Sometimes when a disease has been around for a while, it becomes more virulent. This simply means that it becomes stronger and is resistant to antibiotics or other drugs. It also means that it can make people sicker.

Viruses in infected organism.

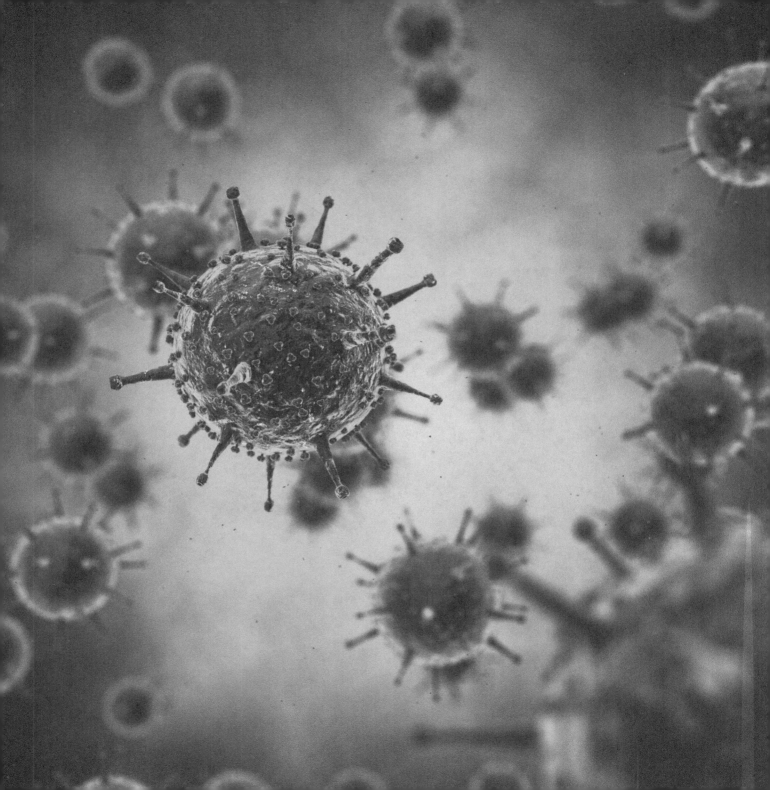

HOW DOES DISEASE SPREAD?

Disease can be spread in a number of different ways. Unsanitary conditions that cause food or drinking water to be unsafe can cause diseases to spread. Examples of diseases that are transmitted this way are:

Flu epidemic. Passengers travel with their faces protectively covered with a mask.

- **CHOLERA,** which causes watery diarrhea and severe vomiting

- **DYSENTERY,** which causes bloody diarrhea

- **TYPHOID FEVER,** which causes severe headaches, stomach pain, and loss of appetite

Another way that disease spreads is through the air. For example, if you have the flu and you cough or sneeze, you can spread the infection to another person.

Boys take water on a street of Kibera, Nairobi, Kenya.

In addition to influenza, which is also called the flu, two other types of diseases that are transmitted in the air are tuberculosis and measles.

Insects frequently carry different types of diseases and can transmit them to large populations of people. For example, mosquitoes can carry malaria and fleas can carry bubonic plague.

Aedes Aegypti mosquitoes with stilt target.

HOW DO EPIDEMICS END?

Epidemics spread rapidly and can kill millions of people. At some point, they do stop, at least for a while, until another outbreak occurs. There are quite a few reasons why an epidemic stops.

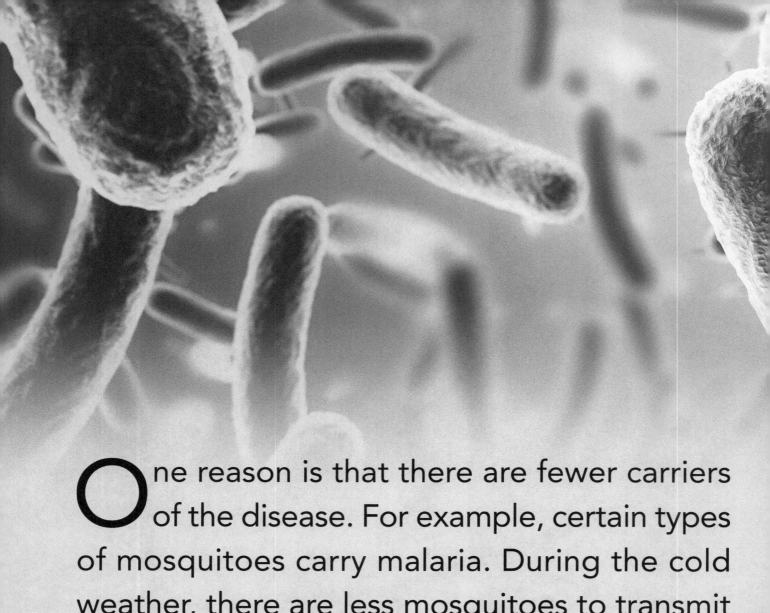

One reason is that there are fewer carriers of the disease. For example, certain types of mosquitoes carry malaria. During the cold weather, there are less mosquitoes to transmit the disease, so this may slow down or stop the cases of malaria.

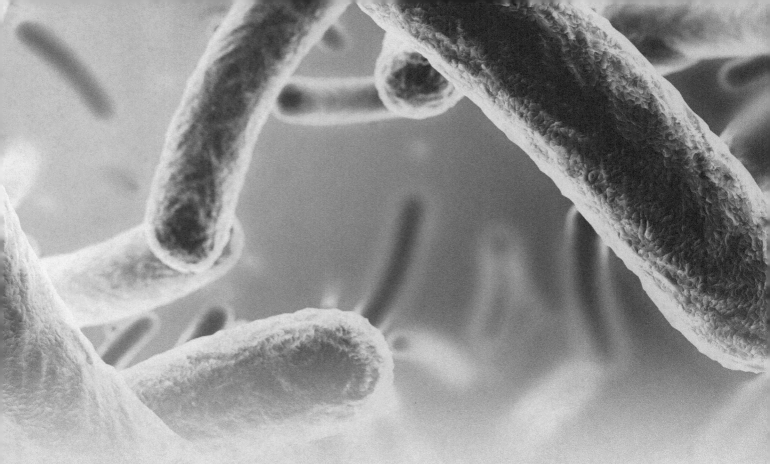

Some types of diseases happen more often during certain times of the year. For example, epidemics of the flu happen in the winter more often than at other times of the year. One reason is that the flu virus survives better in moist air.

Another reason that epidemics eventually die out is because they can't find appropriate hosts. When a disease first strikes, it attacks the weakest people. Babies, elderly people, and adults with weakened immune systems are usually the first to become infected. However, if these people fight off the disease they can build up immunity to it. Over time, the disease finds less and less hosts who are easy to infect.

Fogging to eliminate mosquitoes.

WHAT IS A PANDEMIC?

A pandemic is defined as an epidemic that has infected a large geographic region, such as more than one country, more than one continent, or across the world.

Girl walking wearing a mask in the city street.

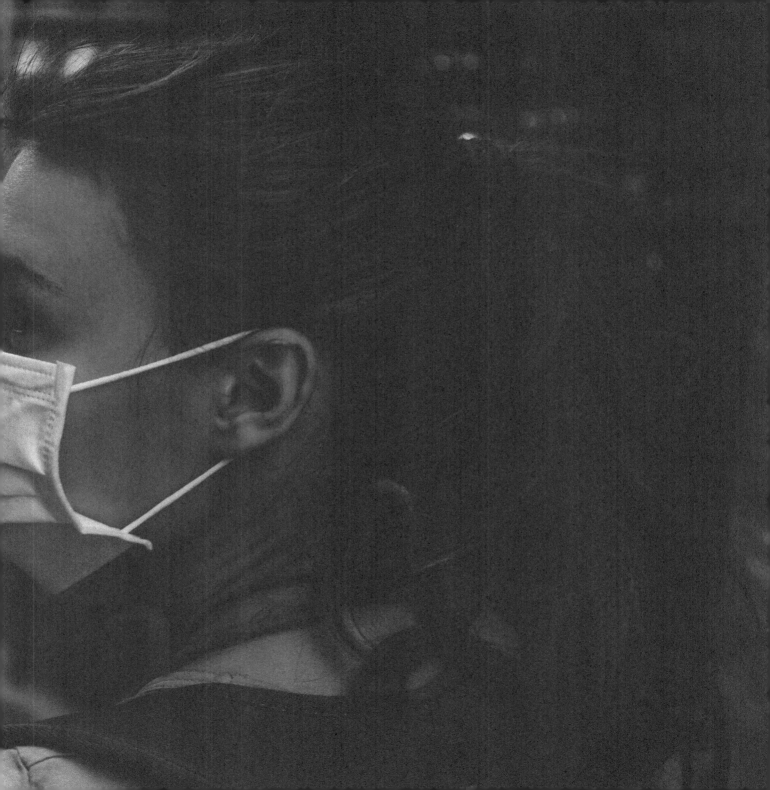

Vaccinating the poor of New York City
against smallpox in 1872.

There are six specific stages of an epidemic that's become a pandemic. These stages have been defined by the World Health Organization, which is a special United Nations agency whose mission is the health of people worldwide.

STAGE 1: The virus is detected in animals. It hasn't been transmitted to humans yet.

STAGE 2: The virus infects humans.

STAGE 3: There are outbreaks of the disease, but it isn't spreading quickly.

STAGE 4: There are human-to-human transmissions of the disease. Whole communities are now infected and the disease has caused an epidemic.

STAGE 5: The virus has spread through one country and is threatening a second country. The disease is moving rapidly and a full-scale pandemic is likely to happen.

STAGE 6: The epidemic is now a full-scale pandemic.

Woman with fever.

THE WORST EPIDEMICS AND PANDEMICS IN HISTORY

There have been many epidemics throughout history and some increased to the size that they were pandemics. Each of them had a huge impact on human history.

Plague doctor.

The Plague of Athens
in 430 BC to 427 BC

This plague began while the city-state of Athens was fighting against the city-state of Sparta. The disease, which most scholars believe was typhoid fever, lingered for over three years. About one fourth of the people living in Athens died including their leader Pericles. Because of the heavy toll of the plague, Athens lost the war against Sparta.

The Plague of Athens.

The Plague of Justinian
in 541 to 542 AD

This plague was one of the first occurrences of the dreaded bubonic plague. It expanded throughout Eastern Europe. At the time, the Emperor Justinian ruled this empire, which was called the Byzantine Empire. During the worst part of the plague, about 5,000 people were dying daily in the city of Constantinople.

Man and women with the bubonic plague with its characteristic buboes on their bodies

Even the emperor himself became ill, but he was able to survive. For the next two centuries, the bubonic plague came back many times. The historical impact of the disease was that the Byzantine Empire couldn't continue its expansion.

Saint Sebastian pleading for the life of a gravedigger afflicted with plague during the 7th-century Plague of Justinian.

The Black Death
from 1347 to 1350 AD

The Black Death pandemic spread through Europe rapidly during the Middle Ages. There wasn't a cure and once it got into people's lungs it was very contagious, which simply means that it transmitted very fast from person to person. At that time, scientists and physicians had no clue how the disease had started. Today it's believed that unsanitary conditions in Asia caused the disease.

The Black Death. Watercolor by Monro S. Orr.

Black rats were infected to start, then, fleas bit them and became infected. The fleas bit humans who subsequently also became infected. However, recent evidence points to gerbils instead of rats as the initial cause of the disease. More than likely, the plague got to Europe from Asia on merchant ships manned by Europeans.

Boccaccio's 'The Plague of Florence in 1348'.

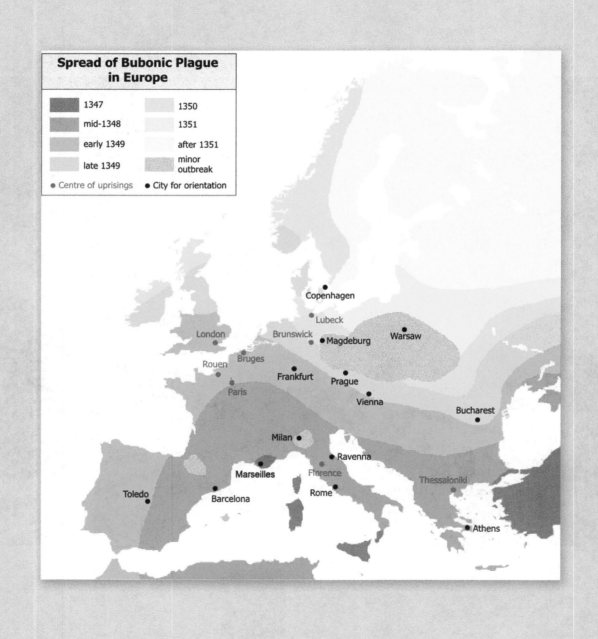

Spread of Bubonic Plague in Europe

- 1347
- mid-1348
- early 1349
- late 1349
- 1350
- 1351
- after 1351
- minor outbreak
- Centre of uprisings
- City for orientation

Copenhagen
Lubeck
London
Brunswick
Magdeburg
Warsaw
Rouen
Bruges
Paris
Frankfurt
Prague
Vienna
Bucharest
Milan
Ravenna
Marseilles
Florence
Thessaloniki
Toledo
Barcelona
Rome
Athens

It's difficult to imagine how frightening the Black Death was. In Paris, more than 800 people were dying every day. There were so many people dying at the same time that their bodies had to be brought to massive pits to be buried.

Map showing the spread of "black death" from Asia towards Europe.

Conditions were very unsanitary during the Middle Ages so there were rats and fleas everywhere. The fleas continued to infect people and once someone got the disease into his lungs he developed a pneumonia form of the disease. Then it was transmitted person to person by coughing and sneezing. The disease caused black- and blue-colored blotches over the skin of its victims as they coughed up blood.

Plague: Carting the Dead, by Moynet.

In Europe and Asia, between 75 million to 200 million people were wiped out by the Black Death. Over 20 million people died in Europe alone, which was over one third of the total population. Today, there are still cases of bubonic plague, but it can be treated with antibiotics so people who become infected can still survive.

Black Rat, Ship Rat.

The bubonic plague came back to Europe numerous times. During the bubonic plague of 1656 AD, doctors wore bird-like masks to protect themselves as they tended to patients. The beaks in these masks had strong fragrances to ward off the horrible smells of the infection.

Image of a plague doctor.

The Spanish Flu
from 1918 to 1920 AD

The influenza virus, known as the Spanish flu, started to spread globally very quickly. Eventually, it infected over 500 million. Of those infected, it's estimated that 50 to 100 million of them were killed.

Demonstration at the Red Cross Emergency Ambulance Station in Washington, D.C., during the influenza pandemic of 1918.

This took place during World War I. Since Spain wasn't fighting in the war, they reported news about the flu and the toll it was taking. Other countries in Europe as well as the United States also had huge outbreaks of the flu, but due to the war they weren't given permission to report on the loss of life in the newspapers.

Walter Reed Hospital flu ward during the Spanish Flu epidemic of 1918-19, in Washington DC.

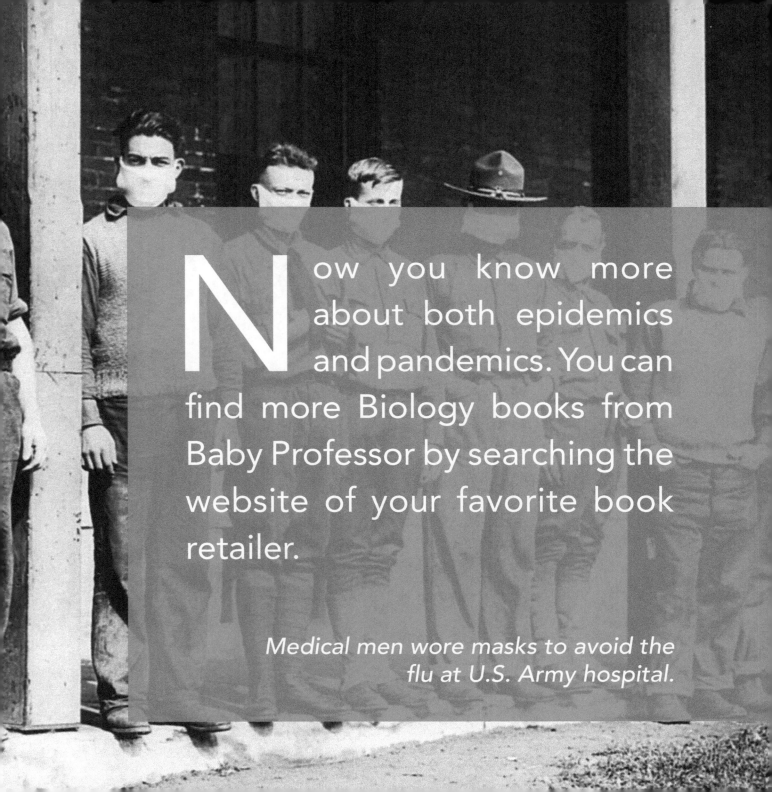

Now you know more about both epidemics and pandemics. You can find more Biology books from Baby Professor by searching the website of your favorite book retailer.

Medical men wore masks to avoid the flu at U.S. Army hospital.

Visit

www.BabyProfessorBooks.com

to download Free Baby Professor eBooks
and view our catalog of new and exciting
Children's Books

CPSIA information can be obtained
at www.ICGtesting.com
Printed in the USA
LVHW061755090520
655285LV00026B/1793